GBAYA

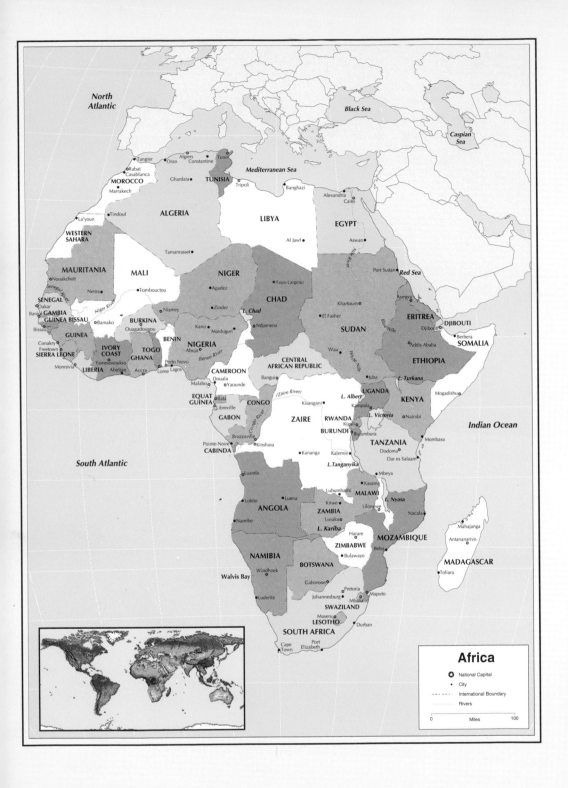

North
Atlantic

Black Sea

Caspian
Sea

Tangier
Algiers
Oran Constantine Tunis
Rabat
Casablanca
MOROCCO   Ghardaïa   TUNISIA
Marrakech   Tripoli   Banghazi
Alexandria
Cairo
La'youn   Tindouf
WESTERN   ALGERIA   LIBYA   EGYPT
SAHARA
Aswan
Tamanrasset   Al Jawf
MAURITANIA   MALI   NIGER   Port Sudan   Red Sea
Nouakchott
Nema   Tombouctou   Agadez   Faya-Largeau   Asmera
SENEGAL   CHAD   ERITREA
Dakar   Niger River   Niamey   Zinder   L. Chad   Khartoum   DJIBOUTI
GAMBIA   Banjul   Bamako   Ndjamena   El Fasher   SUDAN   Djibouti
GUINEA BISSAU   BURKINA   Kano Maiduguri   Addis Ababa   SOMALIA
Bissau   GUINEA   Ouagadougou BENIN   Wau   White Nile   Berbera
Conakry   NIGERIA   ETHIOPIA
Freetown IVORY TOGO   Abuja   CENTRAL   Juba   L. Turkana
SIERRA LEONE COAST GHANA   Benue River   CAMEROON   AFRICAN REPUBLIC
Monrovia Yamoussoukro   Porto Novo   Douala   Bangui   Mogadishu
LIBERIA   Abidjan Accra Lome Lagos   Yaounde   (Zaire River)   UGANDA
Malabo   L. Albert   Kampala   KENYA
EQUAT.   Bata   CONGO   Kisangani   L. Victoria   Nairobi
GUINEA Libreville   ZAIRE   RWANDA   Kigali
GABON   BURUNDI Bujumbura
Brazzaville   Kananga   Kalemie   TANZANIA   Mombasa
Pointe-Noire   Kinshasa   Dodoma
CABINDA   L.Tanganyika   Dar es Salaam
                                                              Mbeya
Luanda   Kasama
Lubumbashi   MALAWI   L. Nyasa
Lobito   Luena   Kitwe   Lilongwe   Nacala
ANGOLA   ZAMBIA   Lusaka
Namibe   L. Kariba
Harare
NAMIBIA   BOTSWANA   ZIMBABWE   MOZAMBIQUE
Bulawayo
Windhoek   Beira
Walvis Bay
Gaborone   Mahajanga
Luderitz   Johannesburg Pretoria   Maputo   Antananarivo
                    Mbabane   MADAGASCAR
SWAZILAND   Toliara
Maseru
LESOTHO   Durban
SOUTH AFRICA
Cape   Port
Town Elizabeth

Mediterranean Sea

South Atlantic

Indian Ocean

Africa

National Capital
City
International Boundary
Rivers

0   Miles   100

The Heritage Library of African Peoples

GBAYA

Philip Burnham, Ph.D.

THE ROSEN PUBLISHING GROUP, INC.
NEW YORK

Published in 1997 by The Rosen Publishing Group, Inc.
29 East 21st Street, New York, NY 10010

First Edition

Manufactured in the United States of America

Library of Congress Cataloging-in-Publication Data

Burnham, P. C., 1942–
    Gbaya / Philip Burnham. — 1st ed.
        p.   cm. — (The heritage library of African Peoples)
    Includes bibliographical references and index.
    ISBN 0-8239-1995-1
    1. Gbaya (African people)—History—Juvenile literature.   2. Gbaya
(African people)—Social life and customs—Juvenile literature.
I. Title.   II. Series.
DT474.6.G32B87   1996
967'.0049636—dc20   96-15575
                                                               , CIP
                                                               AC

Contents

INTRODUCTION

THERE IS EVERY REASON FOR US TO KNOW something about Africa and to understand its past and the way of life of its peoples. Africa is a rich continent that has for centuries provided the world with art, culture, labor, wealth, and natural resources. It has vast mineral deposits, fossil fuels, and commercial crops.

But perhaps most important is the fact that fossil evidence indicates that human beings originated in Africa. The earliest traces of human beings and their tools are almost two million years old. Their descendants have migrated throughout the world. To be human is to be of African descent.

The experiences of the peoples who stayed in Africa are as rich and as diverse as of those who established themselves elsewhere. This series of books describes their environment, their modes of subsistence, their relationships, and their customs and beliefs. The books present the variety of languages, histories, cultures, and religions that are to be found on the African continent. They demonstrate the historical linkages between African peoples and the way contemporary Africa has been affected by European colonial rule.

Africa is large, complex, and diverse. It encompasses an area of more than 11,700,000 square miles. The United States, Europe, and India could fit easily into it. The sheer size is an indication of the continent's great variety in geography, terrain, climate, flora, fauna, peoples, languages, and cultures.

Much of contemporary Africa has been shaped by European colonial rule, industrialization, urbanization, and the demands of a world economic system. For more than seventy years, large regions of Africa were ruled by Great Britain, France, Belgium, Portugal, and Spain. African peoples from various ethnic, linguistic, and cultural backgrounds were brought together to form colonial states.

For decades Africans struggled to gain their independence. It was not until after World War II that the colonial territories became independent African states. Today, almost all of Africa is ruled by Africans. Large numbers of Africans live in modern cities. Rural Africa is also being transformed, and yet its people still engage in many of their customs and beliefs.

Contemporary circumstances and natural events have not always been kind to ordinary Africans. Today, however, new popular social movements and technological innovations pose great promise for future development.

George C. Bond, Ph.D., Director
Institute of African Studies
Columbia University, New York

In the rainy season, savanna grass grows taller than this Gbaya man from Cameroon.

chapter

1

THE PEOPLE

▼ **THE PEOPLE AND THEIR LAND** ▼

The Gbaya (pronounced by-uh) are one of the main cultural groups of northern equatorial Africa. They number about 1 million overall. Gbaya-speakers live in four modern countries, mainly the Central African Republic and Cameroon, with smaller numbers in the Congo Republic and Zaire. These widely scattered Gbaya populations have never been united. Rather, they are divided into many regional sub-groups. Each of these subgroups is in turn divided into many clans called *zu duk*. Members of the same clan consider themselves to be related to a common male ancestor. Today, however, clans no longer recall who their first ancestor was.

The more important Gbaya subgroups are the Mbodomo, Kara, Lai, Dooka, Buli, Bofi, Biyanda, Gbeya, Suma, Ali, Gbanu, Mbusuku, Yangere, Bokare, Yayuwe, and Bokoto. Each of

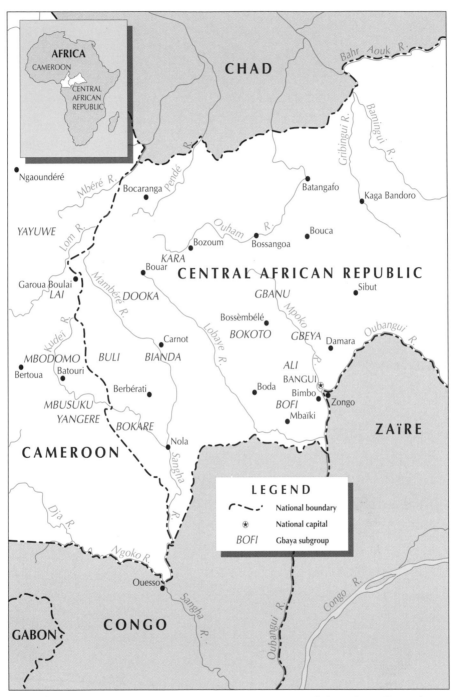

Map of central Africa showing the location of the Gbaya people.

these Gbaya peoples speaks a different version or dialect of the Gbaya language. Some of the dialects are easily understood by speakers of other dialects. However, some dialects are so different that it is difficult for people from different regions to understand each other. The cultures of these Gbaya peoples also differ, but they are similar enough to indicate that the Gbaya groups all have a common origin.

The lands inhabited by the Gbaya lie mainly between four and seven degrees north of the equator. They cover an area of about 120,000 square miles—about one and a half times the size of New York State. With a population of only 1 million people, this area is one of the least populated parts of central Africa. This allows plenty of space for farming, which is the main Gbaya occupation today. In the past, the Gbaya also hunted large and small animals, gathered wild plant foods, and fished in local streams and rivers.

Most of the Gbaya region is a high savanna, or grassland. Small forests are found in the river valleys. There are five months of dry season (November through March), and seven months of rainy season (April through October). Temperatures remain warm throughout the year.

▼ GBAYA HISTORY ▼
We have no written documents or oral

traditions to tell us about the Gbaya's early history. They have probably lived in northern equatorial Africa for centuries. They may have moved temporarily at times when they weren't getting along with their neighbors.

The Gbaya are first mentioned in written history in the 1800s. At that time a *jihad*, or Muslim holy war, was declared by the Fulani leader, Usman dan Fodio, in Nigeria. Fulani warriors attacked what is now northern Nigeria and northern Cameroon. They wanted to convert the indigenous peoples—including the Gbaya—to Islam. The western Gbaya peoples were attacked periodically from the 1840s to the beginning of European colonial rule around 1900. In some areas, Gbaya clans worked together to resist the Muslim warriors. Other Gbaya groups joined the Fulani in their conquests and slave raiding. The Gbaya peoples were not greatly affected by the Atlantic slave trade. However, through contact with the Fulani, they did participate in trans-Saharan slaving. They raided other peoples; occasionally they were raided themselves.

Colonial rule began in the Gbaya region at the very end of the 1800s. The territory of Cameroon was claimed by the Germans. The rest of the Gbaya peoples were incorporated into French equatorial Africa. The first decades of colonial rule were especially hard on the Gbaya.

They were forced into work gangs and faced discrimination.

In the mid-1920s, a Gbaya leader named Karnu became famous. He believed that the Gbaya could free themselves from French and Fulani exploitation by using special rituals that Karnu had learned about in a dream. Many Gbaya believed that Karnu's supernatural power would protect them from French bullets. Many flocked to learn his techniques. There were armed confrontations between Karnu's Gbaya warriors and French soldiers. In 1928, Karnu himself was killed in battle. But Karnu's message was widespread. The Gbaya continued their rebellion against the French until 1930. Karnu's anticolonial movement was an early example of African peoples fighting for their independence. It was one of the largest African independence movements before World War II.▲

chapter

2

SOCIETY

▼ POLITICAL GROUPINGS AND ▼ LEADERSHIP

Gbaya subgroups are divided into numerous clans, or *zu duk*. Before colonial rule, the *zu duk* avoided being ruled by a central government, but they worked together to resist political domination. Clans would join under the command of great leaders to ward off enemies. Otherwise, each Gbaya clan was an independent unit. Neighboring clans sometimes fought over the available natural resources in their region.

Each clan lived in several small, scattered villages, or hamlets, each housing several dozen persons.

Under French colonial rule, small Gbaya hamlets were forced to join together into larger villages. These villages were under the authority of government-appointed headmen. These villages were organized into separate residential zones called *ndok fu* or *nu begara*.

Before colonization, the Gbaya lived in small, scattered villages. French colonizers forced the Gbaya into larger settlements. The village seen here is typical of many Gbaya villages in the savanna today.

In some cases, Gbaya war leaders became permanent chiefs. In the western regions these chiefs formed military and trade links with the Muslim Fulani states. The western Gbaya chiefdoms adopted many of the political customs of the Fulani, but the Gbaya further east resisted this foreign system of government. The Gbaya continued to resist all forms of centralized government well into the colonial period.

▼ MAINTAINING SOCIAL ORDER ▼
Traditional Gbaya villages had no chief. All

The Gbaya do not have a strong tradition of chiefs. However, the French appointed leaders for larger Gbaya villages. At the end of this village road is a chief's house.

elders were considered equal. Because of this it could be difficult to settle disputes in the community. Long-term feuds between families in a village were likely to divide the group. Opposing parties often went their separate ways to start new villages. Since the Gbaya traditionally planted few trees or other permanent crops, they were willing to move to new farmlands, which were readily available in the thinly populated savannas. Today, with the construction of government schools, clinics, wells, and other fixed facilities in many villages, people are not so likely to leave their villages because of a dispute. It does still happen, however.

Many conflicts in Gbaya villages are related to witchcraft. According to Gbaya belief, witchcraft is caused by a substance, known as *dua*, found in the abdomen of certain people. *Dua* gives its carrier the power to harm others. This witchcraft substance is thought to be inherited from a parent.

Despite the harm that may be caused by *dua*, the Gbaya do not believe that this power is necessarily evil. A Gbaya proverb states, "The cleverness of the tortoise is in the tortoise's belly." Some Gbaya folktales portray the tortoise as a trickster who often outwits other animals. In other words, the *dua* in some people's bellies may be used for good as well as for evil. The powers of famous leaders and priests or diviners are thought to come from *dua*.

When misfortune or disputes arise, a member of the village may be suspected of witchcraft. Villagers may consult a *wan gbana*, a person who is thought to have the power to detect witchcraft. If the accused person accepts that his or her *dua* might be causing the misfortune, that person can undergo a ceremony to "cool" the witchcraft force.

In the past, an accused person who insisted that he was innocent might be given a drink made from poisonous tree bark. If he vomited up the poison, he was considered innocent. If he died, he was guilty. The relatives of the accused, however, could contest the verdict. They might demand that there be a search for the actual *dua* in the dead person's belly. If none was found, the accusers might have to pay a large fine, or be ordered to give a child to the dead person's kin group. Today, such poison ordeals and *dua* autopsies are outlawed by the government. Belief in witchcraft is still common among the Gbaya, however. It continues to cause disputes in Gbaya communities.▲

chapter

3

LIVELIHOOD

▼ AGRICULTURE, HUNTING, ▼ AND FISHING

Most Gbaya are farmers. They practice a method known as shifting cultivation. First, trees and vegetation are cleared from a plot of land. Then the land is scorched with a controlled fire. After the soil has been cultivated for several years, it is left fallow for a decade or more. This allows the worn-out soil to become rich and fertile again. Shifting cultivation requires the farmers to move to new farmlands every few years.

Cassava, also called manioc, has been the main staple food crop among most Gbaya peoples since the 1700s. Related to the potato, cassava was brought to central Africa from Brazil by the Portuguese. The Gbaya prepare cassava as a stiff porridge called *kam*, which is eaten with vegetable or meat sauces.

Cassava has a number of advantages over the

Shifting cultivation requires that wooded land be cleared for temporary cultivation. These men are clearing trees to establish a field.

native foods that it replaced, such as millet,
sorghum, and yams. First, it is easier to grow.
This is important because there was always a
shortage of labor in this region. Second, cassava
can be harvested throughout the year. This
means that the crop does not need to be stored
for long periods of time. Fresh tubers may be
dug up whenever needed. This is a good way to
prevent famine. Third, cassava can grow in most
kinds of soil, as long as it has sufficient water.

Other important Gbaya crops include corn,
peanuts, beans, sweet potatoes, and yams.
Cotton was introduced during the French colonial period. It is now the main cash crop in
some areas, especially in the Central African
Republic.

Farmwork in Gbaya society is done by both
men and women. The women do most of the
work. Men clear trees and bush from newly
opened fields, using axes and machetes. Women
are in charge of much of the day-to-day work,
such as planting and weeding. Men and women
each have separate cassava fields. However,
women are expected to dig up the manioc roots
and prepare them by soaking, chopping, drying,
and pounding them into flour, and then sifting
the flour. Most families also have corn fields.
These are worked and harvested by the whole
family.

In the past, the Gbaya spent a great deal of

time hunting to add to their diet. Their region used to be rich in big animals, including elephant, buffalo, leopard, lion, wild pig, and several species of large antelope. Today, although there is no longer much big game, Gbaya still hunt smaller animals, such as duikers and other small antelope, monkeys, baboons, porcupines, cane rats, squirrels, snakes, and birds.

Two main hunting traditions exist among the Gbaya: the individual and the communal. Individuals hunt all year round using spears, crossbows, bows and poisoned arrows, and many varieties of traps. Individual hunting is a daily event without special rules. On the other hand, communal hunting occurs only at certain times of the year. Some Gbaya groups use long nets for their communal hunting. They drive the animals ahead of them to be caught and speared in nets that are hidden in the bush. Other groups of Gbaya use dogs to chase the game toward lines of waiting hunters. Communal hunting is a kind of festival. Able-bodied men leave the village on a day-long hunting expedition. The women spend most of the day preparing a feast to welcome home the hunters.

In addition to farming and hunting, the Gbaya also fish. Just as in hunting, the Gbaya have both individual and communal fishing traditions. Individual fishing with hook and line or traps is something that anyone can do routinely.

When savanna grass is burned to prepare for cultivation, small animals escaping the flames can be easily hunted.

In the past, the whole community held a special fishing event every year. An elder, called the *wan do*, led the event. The community dammed a small river and then threw in crushed herbs that poisoned the fish.

The Gbaya also use other natural products of the forests and savannas for food, medicines, and crafts. They know how to use hundreds of species of plants in their environment. Men gather wild honey. Some even construct hives to attract swarms of wild bees. The honey is used by the women to make *kuri*, a fermented alcoholic drink, which is a seasonal replacement for beer made from corn.

▼ ARTS AND CRAFTS ▼
The Gbaya are skilled in a wide variety of

crafts. In precolonial times, they produced all of the tools and other material things that they needed. Since cotton had not been introduced, cloth was made from the beaten bark of the fig tree. Salt was produced by burning certain plants and extracting salt from the ashes. Soap was made from mixing ashes and fat. The Gbaya were skilled ironworkers. They melted down iron ore in tall furnaces constructed out of mud. The lumps of iron were then converted by Gbaya blacksmiths into hoes, knives, and spear blades. Blacksmiths also made blade-shaped objects used as ceremonial money.

Gbaya women are particularly known for their beautiful pottery. They make large storage jars decorated with shiny black graphite paint. These are often two feet or more in diameter and are made without the aid of a potter's wheel. Traditional Gbaya houses, which are circular in shape, are built by men using local clay in much the same way that women fashion pots: the builders pile up coils of clay to build the walls. The conical roof is made of thatched grass over a framework of poles and vines. This sort of roof keeps out the rain as well as the midday heat.

Gbaya basketry is done by both men and women. Many items are produced by basket-weaving techniques, including mats, woven straw fencing, fish and game traps, shields, beer

Gbaya women are known for their beautiful pottery. These pots were made by Pauline Gbazama and are in the collection of The British Museum.

Today, several vibrant markets exist in Gbaya territory. Local and imported items are available.

buy clothing, household wares, kerosene for their lamps, and other consumer goods.

Since the early 1900s, the Gbaya region has also been the home of Fulani nomads. The Fulani graze their large herds of cattle in the high pastures next to Gbaya villages. They trade their beef, milk, and butter for Gbaya crops. Traditionally, the Gbaya raise goats and chickens, but some have also taken up cattle raising in recent years.▲

4

THE LIFE CYCLE

▼ BIRTH AND CHILDHOOD ▼

Birth among the Gbaya takes place in the mother's house, surrounded by the close family. News of the coming birth is not spread widely in the village. This is to prevent witchcraft or other supernatural dangers from harming the mother or child. Older Gbaya women, or the mother's own mother, act as midwives. They have special knowledge of herbal medicines that ease the birth. The midwives vigorously massage the mother's abdomen to make the baby feel uncomfortable so that it will want to leave the womb. If there is a problem with the birth, the Gbaya believe that the mother may have committed some fault. She is urged to confess publicly. This removes the danger to both herself and her child.

A child is usually named in honor of a senior relative or close friend of the family. The birth of

Family life is central to Gbaya society. Men may marry more than one wife if they can afford it. This Gbaya family is dressed up for a visit to a town. The man's shirt is made from patriotic cloth that celebrates Cameroon.

twins, known as *be dan*, is considered to be a fortunate event. It can, however, bring the risk of supernatural danger to both the parents and the children. Twins in Gbaya society are always given special names—Zari and Gbane for female twins and Ngozo and Tuwe for male twins.

From the time of the twins' birth until they have learned to walk, their parents must observe certain behavioral rules. All four of them must undergo a special purification ceremony in a small hut that is built alongside the family house. On the day of the ceremony, the spirits are invited to enter the house by the blowing of a whistle. The leader of the ceremony takes the

parents and the infant twins into the bush.
There the leaves and bark of certain trees are
collected to be used in a ceremonial bath in a
stream. The wild pepper vine, known as *gaa dan*,
is especially important in this ceremony. Its
Gbaya name can be translated as "peace (of the)
twins." Following the special bath, which washes
away the dangers of twin births, the parents
and babies return to the village for a feast of
celebration.

There are reasons for the precautions taken at
the birth of twins. The Gbaya believe that everyone has a spirit double, known as *dan te*, which
normally remains invisible. When twins are born,
one may represent the spirit double of the other.
To the Gbaya, a twin birth does not happen by
chance. It has been sent by the spirits. If the
parents of twins do not follow the special rules
of behavior regarding twins, their children will
die and return to the spirit world.

Early childhood is mostly a carefree time for
the Gbaya. However, as soon as children can
talk, they begin to learn the rules of good behavior. Children learn to respect their elders, even
if the difference in age is small. In the Gbaya
language, there are separate words for "elder
brother" and "younger brother," as well as
"elder sister" and "younger sister." The order of
birth is very important.

From an early age, Gbaya children begin to

look after their younger brothers and sisters and to do chores for their parents. They go with their parents to the fields and learn about farming. Young boys begin to hunt with small bows and spears made of sticks. It is a proud day when they bring home the first bird or small animal they kill. When girls are seven or eight, they learn how to cook by helping their mothers prepare cassava and other foods.

▼ INITIATION ▼

In traditional Gbaya society, there were many ceremonies to celebrate the different life stages of both men and women. These initiations varied from one Gbaya group to another and could change according to fashion. Today, although many of these initiations have fallen away, initiated persons are still highly respected in Gbaya villages.

Circumcision for boys was carried out at about the age of five. The operation was not accompanied with a special ceremony. The initiation for children of eight to ten years of age was called *diang* for boys and *naayeng* for girls. The child must undergo minor ordeals, such as being rubbed on the buttocks with nettles without crying. The children were also taught special dances and had a feast. These childhood initiations were symbolic for the Gbaya.

An elder named Kombo Banda of the village

of Bouli in Cameroon told the following story about initiation: Children used to wander in nature without food or guidance. They paid no attention to their parents' authority. But one day the parents prepared a large feast for the children and, after the feast, taught them the dance of *diang*. By accepting the food from their parents and by dancing under the direction of their elders, Gbaya children learned about the social ties and moral rules that bind a community together.

These simple childhood initiations were followed by more intensive initiation during teenage years. The *bana* for girls, and the *labi* for boys prepared the initiates for adulthood and marriage. The *bana*, a puberty ceremony practiced by Gbaya Kara groups of the northwestern Central African Republic, was the most difficult of the girls' initiations. It involved physical ordeals as well as training in song, dance, and moral education.

The most widespread of the Gbaya initiations was the *labi*, for boys between the ages of twelve and seventeen. This elaborate ceremony, in its full form, lasted for three years. During this time, the boys lived in a bush encampment separated from the village. As Western-style education came to the area in the 1950s, *labi* initiations conflicted with school attendance. The ceremony was first shortened, and then abolished. Today, the *labi* is practiced only in some of the more remote Gbaya regions in the Central African Republic.

The *labi* began with a ceremony symbolizing the "death" of the boys. They were "speared" by the senior initiator, the *naminga*, while swimming in a small pond. The "dead" boys were dragged from the water by initiated older men and carried off to the bush camp. There they were ceremonially revived. They were scarified on the stomach as a permanent reminder of their *labi* "death." The boys were forbidden to speak the Gbaya language until the end of the initiation period. Instead they had to learn the secret *labi* language reserved for initiated men. They were separated from women and children and were forbidden to reveal the secrets of the *labi* to uninitiated persons. Each boy was given a *labi* name or title. This indicated his particular role in the initiation camp and dances.

During the period of *labi* initiation, the boys were given lessons in hunting and bushcraft, and trained for their life as adult members of the community. They were taught many songs in the *labi* language and trained in rigorous dances. At the end of their long period of initiation, the boys returned to the village. There they performed their elaborate dances in public. They were showered with gifts from their relatives,

Feasting is an important part of Gbaya celebrations. These men prepare a slaughtered cow for a feast.

and their mothers prepared a feast to celebrate their rebirth as adult men.

▼ MARRIAGE AND DIVORCE ▼

Marriage among the Gbaya is not just a union between two people; it is also a union between two kin groups. The Gbaya forbid marriages between members of the same clan, or *zu duk*, as well as between individuals who are related in any way. Each family wants its child's spouse to be of good character and hardworking. Prior to marriage, each family makes sure that there is no history of witchcraft in the other family. The betrothal period lasts for a year or more so that the parents can be sure they have found a good match for their child.

Gbaya girls are considered ready for marriage once they have reached puberty. Most will be engaged by the age of sixteen. Gbaya boys wait until they are somewhat older, usually eighteen or nineteen. When a boy has found a girl he wishes to marry, he will show his intentions by giving a gift of a chicken or other meat to the girl's parents. If the girl and her parents are prepared to allow the boy to court her, they will prepare the gift as a meal for themselves. If they do not agree, they will return the gift uneaten.

A boy who is regarded as an acceptable suitor must begin to make bridewealth payments. These payments include money, cooking pans, pieces of cloth, goats, machetes, hoes, and spears. After these items are received, they are divided among the girl's parents and relatives. The amount of the bridewealth is negotiated by the families. It usually takes the suitor several years to pay in full. Today, the total amount can cost the equivalent of $100 or more, which is 25 to 50 percent of a typical Gbaya person's annual income. For a boy's first marriage, his father is likely to pay most of the bridewealth for his son.

During the engagement, the boy must also perform brideservice for his future

parents-in-law. He spends several periods of a
week or more at the girl's village. There he helps
with farmwork, wood cutting, and house build-
ing. He also goes hunting with the girl's father.
During these visits, he is allowed to enjoy meals
with his fiancée. While the young man is in
brideservice, the girl's parents will observe their
future son-in-law carefully. If he does not seem
to be a good worker, the girl's parents may
decide to repay the bridewealth and not give
their daughter to him.

Often a girl has several suitors at one time.
They all compete during the brideservice period
to win the favor of the girl. Eventually, she and
her parents will pick one of the boys and return
the bridewealth payments to the others. Today,
Gbaya girls have more control over the choice of
their husbands than in the past. Gbaya parents
usually let their daughter marry the man of her
choice.

During the betrothal period, the girl visits
her prospective husband's village. There she
helps his mother with chores around the house
and shows what a good wife she will make.
Since the girl will move in with her husband's
family after marriage, they are particularly con-
cerned to see that she is hardworking and
respectable.

The future husband must build a new
house near the other homes of his family and

plant new fields for him and his wife. The young
man must now settle down and become a
responsible household head.

Many Gbaya fathers today complain that
their sons do not take the preparation for marriage seriously enough. Fathers also complain
that the older generation has lost control over
the younger generation. They believe that this is
because there is no longer a *labi* initiation, which
used to train boys to become adults. Gbaya
youths in the rural areas today are attracted by
the more modern lifestyle of the towns and
cities, which they learn about in school, on the
radio, and from visitors to the village. Before
settling down to a life of marriage and farming
in the village, young Gbaya men often travel to
town, where they visit relatives and seek paid
employment.

The marriage of a new couple occurs when
all the preparations to welcome the new bride to
her husband's village are complete. The young
man's family celebrates by having a feast.
Moving away from home and joining her in-
laws' village is a difficult transition for many
Gbaya girls. Her husband must show his respect
and support for his new wife or she may run
away, back to her own family.

The birth of the couple's first child is a happy
event in their marriage. Should the couple not
have children after a year or two, they may

Kam, a stiff porridge made from cassava, is the main food of most Gbaya.
It is always served at celebrations, such as weddings.

decide to divorce. Other common causes of divorce include adultery and domestic violence. In the event of divorce, the wife's parents must pay back all of the bridewealth that they received at the time of the marriage. Because this repayment is often difficult, the families try to encourage the couple to settle their differences and stay together. The Gbaya marriage is seen as an important linkage between two family groups and not, as in other societies, mainly a personal relationship between the husband and wife.

A woman marrying into her husband's village is at first viewed as an outsider (called *koo kana,* "stranger woman"). As she bears children for her husband's family, she gains acceptance into the family. Older women who have had many children are highly respected members of the community. They may take on important roles in the community's ceremonial life.

Wealthy men in Gbaya society may sometimes practice polygyny, that is, marry more than one wife. In this way, they demonstrate their social status, father more children, and head a larger household. Women's attitudes toward polygyny vary considerably. In some cases, a first wife welcomes the arrival of a second one. The two women share the work and keep each other company. More often, however, a first wife discourages her husband from taking another wife, fearing that a second wife and her new children will compete for her husband's attention. Today, polygyny is becoming less common, but it is still practiced. Women are not the only ones opposing it. Men are also finding that it is increasingly difficult to support more than one wife.

▼ AGING AND DEATH ▼

Age brings greater status for men and women in Gbaya society. As long as elders remain mentally alert, their words command great respect. As senility sets in, however, the elderly are treated more and more like children. They are looked after and fed, but are also made fun of for their mental lapses. They are seen as ready to join the world of the ancestral spirits. When death eventually comes to them, their funerals are a mixture both of sadness for their departure and of celebration for their achievements and long life.

The elder's body is buried on the day of death in the courtyard of his house, accompanied by drumming, mock battles, and hunts performed by his friends. These symbolize his great deeds in life and are meant to honor him. The dead man's children are then called to the graveside. At the time of his death, the man's children rub their faces with charcoal. This prevents his spirit from recognizing them and cursing them for any hard words that may have come between them. Each child now throws a piece of charcoal into the grave. The pieces of charcoal are counted to determine how many children the man had.

Next, the man's eldest son picks up a shield and declares, "I will take over for you. Go well!" Then the period of the funeral known as *nana gore* ("female relatives of the dead") begins. The dead man's younger brother collects the spears of all the mourners and sticks them in the ground. He then says that those present should "pull the spears out of the ground to see what happens."

Anyone who pulls a spear from the ground is declaring his friendship for the dead man. But it is also at this moment that certain members of the dead man's family may blame other relatives for the man's death through witchcraft. The sisters and daughters of the dead elder often blame his wife. As a *koo kana*, a "stranger woman" to the village, she is not trusted. The suspected person may be ritually, that is symbolically, beaten by the dead man's female relatives.

When it is an aged person who has died, this *nana gore* ritual is done partly in jest. However, when it is a younger person who has died, the ritual is likely to be much more serious, because witchcraft is usually suspected as the cause of death. Few deaths in Gbaya society are thought to be due to natural causes alone. When a person is killed by snakebite or crushed by a falling tree while preparing a field, the Gbaya usually suspect that a witch was the deeper cause behind the accident.

Following the day of the funeral, the widow (or widower) enters a period of mourning known as *gera*. During this time, he or she eats little and does not wash. This period lasts for three days in the case of a man's death and four days for a woman's. (The Gbaya consider the number three as the "male" number and four as the "female" number.)

During *gera*, the dead person's spirit is thought to be lurking in the bush nearby. The surviving spouse uses certain herbs to keep the dead person's spirit from returning to the house. At the end of the *gera*, the surviving spouse must remove the dangerous "pollution" of death, known as *simbo*. Certain plants are used in a ritual bath to "cool" the danger of *simbo*. Following this ceremonial washing, the surviving spouse returns to regular daily life. However, he or she must continue to observe special rules of behavior for a year, until the full mourning period has ended.

Some elders are especially important in their communities, or have earned reputations as great hunters, or, in the past, as great warriors. The family of such an elder may decide to commemorate his deeds several years after his death. The family holds a second funeral celebration,

The Gbaya use large drums during many ceremonies and celebrations. They play a key role in the *gbanga fio*, a second funeral celebration.

known as *gbanga fio*. Guests are invited from far and wide, and large quantities of food and corn beer are prepared for this feast. The eldest son of the dead man leads the ceremony, and there is dancing to the beat of large drums. At the end of the several days of celebration, the dead man's nephew (the son of his sister) sacrifices a goat or chicken beside the largest drum. He makes a short speech to the assembled crowd, asking the dead man to bless his living relatives.▲

5

WORLDVIEW, RELIGION, AND PHILOSOPHY

GBAYA TRADITIONAL RELIGION INCLUDES A creator god, So e wi, along with various lesser spirits, *so*.

In this religion, human beings themselves are believed to be made up of several spiritual aspects. There is *omi*, "breath," which disappears at death. *Dan te*, literally "friend of the body," also called *so te*, "spirit of the body," is the spiritual essence of the person. It is this part that becomes an ancestor after death. *Giyo te*, a person's shadow, is an extension of a person and is sometimes associated with *so te*. *Ho te*, "phantom," is the part of a person that leaves the body during sleep and roams around.

The seat of a person's emotions and senses, according to the Gbaya, is in the liver, *se*. Many words that the Gbaya use to express their feelings contain this term. For example, *yim se*, "anger," literally means "pain in the liver," while *dang se*, "sorrow," literally means "bad liver."

So e wi, the creator, is a distant god that is not involved in day-to-day affairs. When Gbaya try to influence events through prayer or sacrifice, they first call upon the spirits of close male or female ancestors, *so da* and *so na*.

There were no specialized priests or religious organization in traditional Gbaya society. All religious actions were carried out at the family or village level. In traditional religion, which is still followed today, the eldest son of a deceased man prays to his ancestors on behalf of his own immediate family and the families of his younger brothers. He sacrifices a chicken on an altar behind his house from time to time, asking his ancestors to give him and his relatives abundant food and good health.

At the beginning of the dry season, a senior elder leads the whole village in an annual sacrifice. He prays to the spirit of the place, *so kao*, while standing next to the large rock or tree where it lives. *So kao* is thought to control success in agriculture and hunting in the area. Sometimes a village suffers from poor crops or bad hunting, and sacrifices to *so kao* do not improve the situation. Then the village may decide to move its location, since "the *kao* has been ruined" in that place.

In addition to these regular prayers, the

Leaves from the *sore*, the Gbaya "peace tree," are used in several Gbaya ceremonies. Here they can be seen attached to the rear of the figure on the left.

Gbaya also perform several ceremonies to counteract bad luck or to settle disputes that are troubling the village. The ceremonies *zanga nu* and *pi gangmo* both use water and tree leaves to "cool" the heat of supernatural dangers and to end arguments. As a Gbaya proverb declares, "A place of quarrels is a place of death." The Gbaya believe that arguments between members of the same village not only cause tensions, which may split the village apart, but can also bring curses against the place. In the *pi gangmo* ceremonies, a senior woman of the village plays a prominent role. She uses the leaves of the Gbaya "peace tree," *sore*, along with other ingredients, to purify and "cool" members of her village.

The Gbaya think that certain actions are contaminated with supernatural danger. Many Gbaya ceremonies are designed to wash away the *simbo*, or "dirt," of quarrels, fear, pollution, and death. Certain animals, such as the leopard and the eland (a large antelope), and people who were killed in war are thought of as carriers of *simbo*. A hunter or a warrior who has killed a *simbo* animal or person must undergo a cleansing ceremony before returning to his village.

Although many elements of Gbaya traditional religion are still observed today, Gbaya have now been in contact with Islam and Christianity for many years. Most Gbaya have been converted to one of these world religions. Sometimes aspects of traditional religion are combined with Islam or Christianity.

Islam was brought to the Gbaya by the Fulani during their *jihad*, or holy war, in the 1800s. Islam is still strongly used among the Gbaya groups in the northwest.

Today, many Gbaya are members of various Christian churches, including Lutheran, Catholic, Baptist, Adventist, and Pentecostal. American and French missionaries began the conversion of the Gbaya to Christianity. Now many Gbaya have themselves been trained as pastors. Since there is no traditional Gbaya chief in a village, Gbaya pastors often play leading roles in their communities today.▲

6

MUSIC AND ORAL LITERATURE

▼ MUSIC ▼

Music and dance are important parts of Gbaya daily life. However, there are no professional musicians in Gbaya society. From early childhood, all Gbaya participate in communal singing and dancing. Children play the various Gbaya musical instruments—drums, thumb pianos (the *sanza* or *timbiri*), mouth-harps, rattles, and, in some areas, xylophones.

Those who have the skill and motivation continue to practice on their own. As adults they may gain a reputation in the village or region for their talent. These people are often called upon at feasts, dances, and ceremonies to play their instruments and lead the singing. They perform both well-loved traditional songs and pieces that they have composed themselves.

Today, many young Gbaya still learn to play traditional instruments and sing traditional

SOME GBAYA PROVERBS

Insects must join hands to cross the river—People can accomplish large tasks if they cooperate.

If the *banga bingi* vine grows out of the forest into the savanna, the bush fire may come—A person who cuts oneself off from his or her relatives risks getting into trouble.

If you show off your strength, battle will find you—People who brag are liable to get into trouble.

The ax that cuts the wood will not be left alone at the fire—A hardworking person will be popular in the village.

Young girls conquer advice—Said of children who refuse to listen to good advice.

Gbaya songs. However, they also have access to the radio and are interested in other styles of music from all over the world. Homemade guitars are now commonly seen in Gbaya villages. Modern African, Afro-Caribbean, and American musical styles are very popular.

▼ ORAL LITERATURE ▼

Most of the traditional wisdom and morals of

THE TALE OF EAR AND MOSQUITO

Once upon a time there was Ear and Mosquito. After working for a long time they were going home and stopped by a stream. They took off their clothes and Mosquito said to Ear, "Ear, since you can hear so well, if you hear the voices of people coming down to the stream to draw water, be sure to tell me. My legs are so pale, I'm so thin, and my belly is so flat. I don't want them to see me."

After they had bathed for a while, Ear heard the voices of people approaching. He quickly dressed and climbed up and sat on the bank. "Uncle! Uncle! Have you heard the voices of people coming?" asked Mosquito. But Ear answered: "No, no one is coming."

So Mosquito continued to bathe. All of a sudden, he raised his eyes and . . . My goodness, there were people! This was too much and he said, "Uncle, you have played a horrible trick on me. To pay you back, I'm never going to leave you. For ever and ever, when you are sleeping, I'll come and go buzz-buzz-buzz-buzz beside you. I'm never going to leave you alone." This is my little tale. It is I, Bello André, of Betare Oya.

Gbaya society are passed from one generation to the next through folktales, proverbs, and other forms of oral literature. These traditions are usually communicated in the evening as the family group gathers at home. Some Gbaya men and women become famous storytellers, captivating audiences with their amusing and clever style.

A Gbaya tale usually has a song in the middle. The storyteller leads the audience in call-and-response verses that are accompanied by a rhythm, beat out with gourds or bottles. Anyone can join in the storytelling. Even children are encouraged to take their turn with simple stories, such as the tale of Ear and Mosquito, told by Bello André, a child living in the village of Betare Oya (see opposite page).

The main characters of many Gbaya tales are animals. There are also characters like Gbaso, an ogre-like creator spirit whom other characters try to outwit. Another important character is Wanto. His name in Gbaya means both "spider" and also "the master (*wan*) of the tale (*to*)." Wanto is a human-like trickster who is often tripped up by his own tricks. He sometimes has to be helped or rescued by his more level-headed wife, Laiso. (A tale involving these characters is on pages 54–55.)

Gbaya folktales are not the only source of moral lessons which parents and grandparents relate to children. The Gbaya have a rich store of proverbs that they use constantly in daily conversation and in public speeches to instruct a listener. Many proverbs require a deep knowledge of Gbaya culture to fully understand them. Others, however, refer to values that are universally understood.▲

THE TALE OF WANTO, GBASO, AND THE ORIGIN OF FOOD

Long ago, in the beginning, there was a large silk-cotton tree. Inside it lived Gbaso, who was very rich. He owned all the foods in the world, and kept all the plants and animals captive in his tree. Only Tortoise, Hare, Wanto, and Wanto's wife Laiso lived outside the tree. They only had roots to eat.

When Gbaso went out from the tree, all his captives accompanied him. To leave the tree, Gbaso blew on a whistle named Fel to open the door. Gbaso kept the whistle hidden near the entrance to the tree.

One day, Wanto was hiding near the tree and saw Gbaso go out and hide the whistle, but Wanto didn't yet understand the use of the whistle. So he waited until the evening for Gbaso to come back. When he saw Gbaso blow the whistle to open the door, Wanto figured out a plan to get inside the tree.

The next day, Wanto returned to the tree and waited for Gbaso and his people to leave. Wanto called his companions, blew the whistle to open the door, and led his excited friends into the tree. There they ate and drank to their hearts' content. You know Wanto: When there is something to eat, he doesn't want to leave even the tiniest morsel behind!

Wanto and his friends were so busy eating that they completely lost track of the time. Suddenly, they heard Gbaso and the others coming home. In a panic, Wanto and his friends looked for hiding places. Wanto hid in a granary, clutching food that he had stolen. Tortoise transformed himself into a grindstone, Hare hid under Gbaso's bed, and Laiso hid in the bush nearby.

The wife of Gbaso had grilled some peanuts, and she began to grind them with a flat rock, using Tortoise's back as a grindstone. Tortoise began to moan in pain. Gbaso's wife continued her work, believing that this noise came from outside. The cries of Tortoise grew louder and he began to sing:

Ouch, my back! The back of Tortoise.
Hare is under the bed; Laiso is in the bush.
Wanto is in the granary . . .

The woman ran out and called her friends. "The grindstone is speaking!" They came to listen but heard nothing and told the woman to go back to her work. But the pain made Tortoise sing again:

Ouch, my back! The back of Tortoise . . .

Then everyone understood there were strangers in their tree. The men armed themselves and seized Hare and Laiso. They placed a ladder against the granary, but Wanto had set nooses near the entrance. One by one he trapped each of his attackers and tied them up tightly. Soon only Gbaso was left, but he was much too strong for Wanto. So Wanto threw red pepper into Gbaso's eyes and blinded him temporarily.

Wanto freed his companions and cried, "May all the foods come out of this tree and spread over the earth!" By the time Gbaso recovered, all the foods were gone.

chapter

7

THE GBAYA TODAY

THE GBAYA PEOPLE HAVE EXPERIENCED
many changes since the 1800s. Their lifestyle is
changing even more quickly today. Although
most Gbaya still live in rural areas, hunting is no
longer as important as it once was. This is partly
because large wild animals have become scarce.
Gbaya men and women still farm most of their
own food. However, they now grow corn and
cassava specifically to sell for money.

Cash income has become more important for
the Gbaya over the last several decades. They
need money to pay school fees, pay for medical
care, build modern-style housing, and purchase
consumer goods, such as radios, bicycles and
motorcycles, sewing machines, and many other
products. However, the national economies in
the countries in which the Gbaya live—Central
African Republic, Cameroon, the Congo
Republic, and Zaire—are in crisis and have

Many changes have occurred in Gbaya society in the last 100 years.
Their villages are no longer as widely scattered as they once were. The savanna
(above) has undergone many changes and there is less land available for
agriculture. Trade and markets (below) have become increasingly important.

Many rural Gbaya experience poverty. For families like the one seen here, cash income has become vital in order to pay for education and get ahead in the modern economies of the African countries where the Gbaya live today.

increasing international debts. It is difficult for the Gbaya and other peoples to maintain their standard of living.

Most Gbaya children receive at least some Western-style schooling, but there are many more boys in school than there are girls. Fewer than 10 percent of Gbaya children progress beyond primary school. Educational facilities are still poor in most Gbaya areas. Many rural families have trouble meeting the cost of sending a child to school. The few Gbaya who have a high school or university education mainly find jobs as government teachers, policemen, soldiers, health workers, or office employees. Some enter a business career or pursue a profession, such as law or medicine.

The Gbaya have a fairly large population in both the Central African Republic and Cameroon. However, the fact that most Gbaya live outside the main cities has kept them from having great influence in national politics. Although Gbaya representatives are regularly elected in Gbaya districts, it is only in the last few years that Gbaya leaders have won high-level political offices in national government.

Many Gbaya believe that their people have not been fairly represented in national politics. Recently a group of activists in Cameroon formed a national association of Gbaya people, known as MOINAM. This organization, which holds regular meetings, promotes Gbaya culture. It hopes to give Gbaya people a strong voice in regional and national affairs. MOINAM especially tries to educate Gbaya youth about their own history and traditions. Many elders feel that young Gbaya are too attracted to modern lifestyles and are not well-informed about their own culture.

This is a conflict for the younger generation of many African peoples. How should they balance their desire for an improved standard of living and more modern lifestyle with a commitment to their own cultural heritage? Should they identify more strongly with their own

The Gbaya once placed no emphasis on having leaders. This Gbaya chief's compound is an example of how much their culture has changed. Today, the Gbaya, like most people in the world, have to find ways to balance their traditions with their hopes for the future.

people or with their modern nations? These are the questions that the Gbaya face as they enter the twenty-first century.▲

Glossary

dua Substance found in the abdomen of certain people that allows them to practice witchcraft.

fallow A period in which land is not farmed.

kam Food; a stiff cassava porridge.

kuri An alcoholic drink prepared from honey.

MOINAM Gbaya cultural association in Cameroon.

omi A person's breath; the spiritual life force.

ordeal A physical test, often dangerous.

polygyny Practice of having more than one wife at the same time.

se Liver; the source of emotions.

simbo Supernatural danger.

so Spiritual being or god.

So e wi Creator spirit.

so te A person's spirit.

sore Tree used in ceremonies.

taboos Special rules of behavior.

thumb piano A small instrument with keys that are plucked with the thumbs.

zu duk Clan; people related to the same male ancestor.

For Further Reading

The few sources that exist on the Gbaya are challenging reading.

Burnham, P. *Opportunity and Constraint in a Savanna Society: The Gbaya of Meiganga, Cameroon.* London: Academic Press, 1980.

————. *The Politics of Cultural Difference in Northern Cameroon.* Washington, DC: Smithsonian Institution, 1996.

Burnham, P., and Christensen, T. "Karnu's Message and the 'War of the Hoe Handle': Interpreting a Central African Religious Movement." *Africa,* Vol. 53, No. 4, 1983, pp. 3–22.

Christensen, T. *An African Tree of Life.* Maryknoll: Orbis Books, 1990.

DeLancey, M. *Cameroon: Dependence and Independence.* Boulder: Westview Press, 1989.

Kalck, P. *Historical Dictionary of the Central African Republic.* Metuchen, NJ: Scarecrow Press, 1980.

Noss, P., ed. *Grafting Old Rootstock: Studies in Culture and Religion of the Chamba, Duru, Fula, and Gbaya of Cameroon.* Dallas: International Museum of Cultures, 1982.

Index

ABOUT THE AUTHOR
Currently Professor of Social Anthropology at University College in London, Philip Burnham has also taught at universities in France and Nigeria. He studied Anthropology and African Studies at Cornell University and the University of California at Los Angeles. Dr. Burnham has been conducting research among the Gbaya since 1968, and has written several books and numerous articles on African societies.

PHOTO CREDITS: All photographs by Philip Burnham, Ph.D., except p. 25, © The British Museum and p. 23, photographer unknown (courtesy of Philip Burnham).

CONSULTING EDITOR: Gary N. van Wyk, Ph.D.

LAYOUT AND DESIGN: Kim Sonsky